Long Beach

Clayoquot

and Beyond

Long Beach,

Clayoquot

and Beyond

TEXT BY BRIAN PAYTON
PHOTOGRAPHY BY BOB HERGER

RAINCOAST BOOKS
Vancouver

For Lily
— B.P.

For Megan
— B.H.

First published in 1997 by

Raincoast Books
8680 Cambie Street
Vancouver, B.C.
V6P 6M9
(604) 323-7100

1   3   5   7   9   10   8   6   4   2

CANADIAN CATALOGUING IN PUBLICATION DATA

Payton, Brian, 1966–
Long Beach, Clayoquot and beyond

ISBN 1-55192-063-8

1. Long Beach Region (B.C.) – Guidebooks. 2. Clayoquot Sound Region (B.C.) –
Guidebooks. 3. Vancouver Island (B.C.) – Guidebooks.
I. Herger, Bob. II. Title.
FC3844.2.P39 1997   917.11'2   C96-910695-5
F1089.V3P39 1997

Designed by Dean Allen
Project Editor: Michael Carroll
Copy Editor: Joanne Richardson
Map by Eric Leinberger

Printed and bound in China through Palace Press International

*Raincoast Books gratefully acknowledges the support of the
Canada Council, the Department of Canadian Heritage,
and the British Columbia Arts Council.*

TITLE PAGE: *Aerial view of Radar Beach, Cox Point,
and the southern end of Clayoquot Sound. This area of Vancouver Island
is the ancestral home of the Nuu-chah-nulth people,
whose name means "all along the mountains."*

Contents

Map 7

Preface 9

Introduction: *Seashore Sanctuary* 13

Surf City, Canada 17

Staking a Claim at Florencia Bay 25

Local Forecast: *Ever-Changing Moods* 33

Rainforest Reflections 41

People of Salmon and Cedar 49

Transforming Tofino 53

Meares Island: *Sentinel of the Sound* 65

A Clayoquot Discovery 71

Last Stop, Ucluelet 81

If You Go 87

Selected Reading 92

Notes on the Photography 96

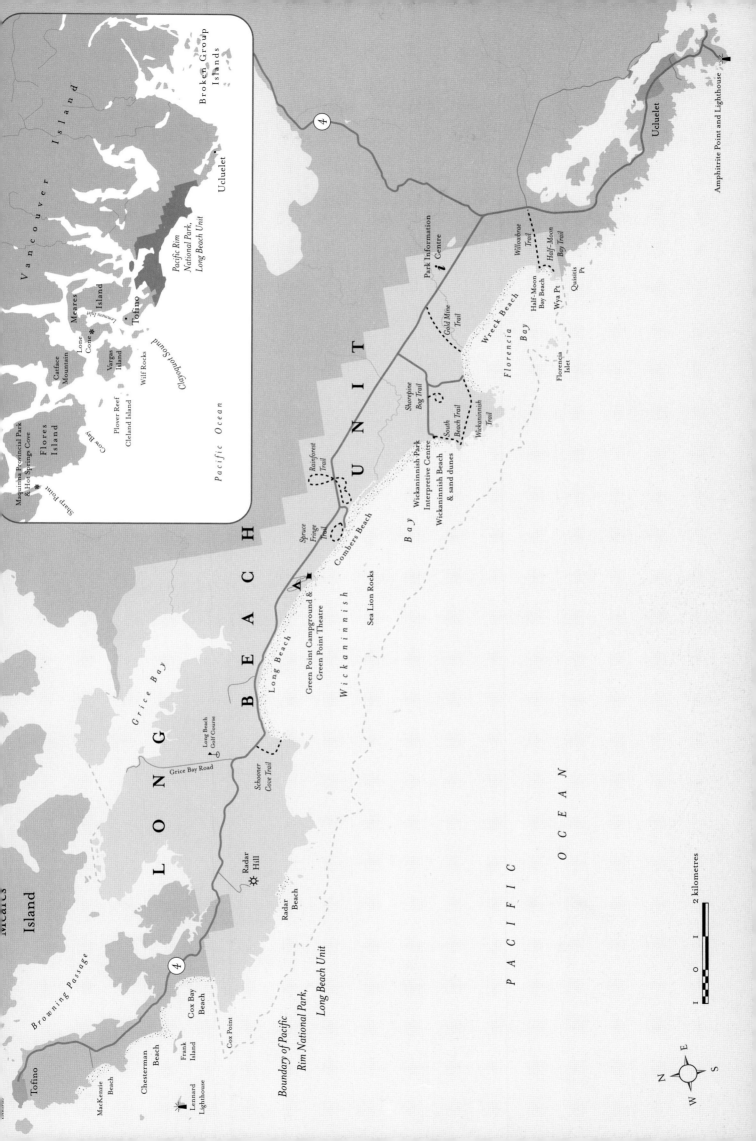

Preface

A beach is a strip of sand separating dry land from sea. It may change shape with the turn of the tide, and it may change personality in foul weather and fair, but it is still just a strip of sand. As though it were a blank canvas, people colour the beach with their own memories and dreams until it takes on a deeply personal character. Few tracts of barren territory mean so much to so many.

There is a strip of sand on the exposed west coast of Canada's Vancouver Island that invites superlatives. Long Beach is both the name of a beach and one of the three "units" of Pacific Rim National Park Reserve. It leads to a series of other long beaches, the village of Tofino, and the shore of Clayoquot Sound. Here, the crashing surf meets the ancient rainforest, eagles soar above passing whales, and children skip barefoot along the endless shore. Here, nature's fragile beauty and awesome power converge in one of North America's most captivating places.

With this collection of words and images, Bob Herger and I have endeavoured to capture the spirit of this place. Our goal was not to create a guidebook or historical account of the region — both have already been done. Instead, we set out to profile one of our favourite places as we have come to see it and to give you a sense of what it is like to be there. We have enjoyed creating this book and filling in that blank strip of sand. It is our privilege to share this experience with you.

This book would not have been possible without the help, encouragement, and guidance of many friends, both old and new. We would especially like to thank: Sean Gibbs (for the inaugural ride); Dave Pettinger; Erica Mclellan; Maureen Houlihan; Allister Fernie; Phebe Nelson; John Launstein; Natalie, Carolyn, and Stephie; Ken Budd; Tom Ellison; Mike Fernie; Shad Evans; Marj and Bill Herger; Monty Little; Brian Johnston; Richard from Remote Passages; Shaun Goddard; the staff of Western Canoeing; Paul Good; Mike Remek; Kim Murphy; Mark and Carol Oun; Sea Trek Expeditions; Antje Egenolf; Bill McIntyre; Marcel Gijssen; Kara-Lynn Bragg; and, finally, the team at Raincoast — Mark Stanton, Michael Carroll, and Dean Allen — for their vision, finesse, and style.

A jogger's footprints are the only signs of human presence on a glorious morning on Chesterman Beach.

NEXT PAGE: *All alone at sunup with Long Beach, Lovekin Rock, and the big blue beyond.*

Seashore Sanctuary

When we first pulled into the parking lot at the north end of Long Beach, I could scarcely believe my eyes. The wide, sandy beach stretched out before us beyond the limits of imagination. The lush green rainforest crowded the surrounding hills, and Lovekin Rock, awash in blue sky and sea, was wading just offshore. And there, right out in front of us in the rising swell, were the promised surfers. My God, it was all true.

The day before, in the musty confines of the sports equipment room at the University of Victoria, I found myself staring incredulously at a giant surfboard sticking out from behind the hockey nets, tents, and canoes. The guy in charge confirmed the unbelievable rumour: that up the coast of Vancouver Island — where the land meets the uninterrupted Pacific swell — there was surfing in the Great White North. This I had to see. I enlisted a friend, packed the board, and headed up-island.

We got out of our little red Rabbit, hopscotched across the mass of driftwood logs, and landed squarely on the sand of Long Beach. We took off our shirts. The warm sun and the sound of the tumbling breakers worked their hypnotic effect. Eventually I pulled on an ill-fitting dive suit, picked up that ancient surfboard, and strode toward the sea. Before that moment I had never been out past the shore break, let alone on top of a surfboard. But as I felt the waves wash up around my ankles, I knew that this was the start of an enduring affair.

Over the dozen years since that sun-drenched afternoon, I have been returning to Long Beach. I come to ride the waves, camp out on the sand, and stare up at the Milky Way splashed bright across the nighttime sky. I quickly learned that my first semitropical day was more the exception than the rule. Located on the border between the Pacific Ocean and the temperate rainforest, Long Beach experiences stints of relentless rain and mighty winter storms. But, oh, those sunny, summer days. Made more precious by their transience, they stay in the mind forever.

Long Beach is where many people get their first glimpse of the open ocean. Every summer I see little kids squirm out of their parents' arms, skip to the water's edge, then run back as if they are being chased by a sea monster. Eventually they all dip their toes into the world's largest ocean — just as their parents did before them, just as kids on Japanese and Russian shores are doing at the very same moment.

There are countless ways in which people interact with this place. Some come to explore the teeming tide pools, fly kites, paddle canoes, or just read magazines in the summer sun; others come to catch the springtime parade of passing whales, weather the winter storms, or just hold hands and watch the sun go down on Canada. But for me, it all comes back to the waves. I am happiest sitting on my board out past the breakers on the incoming tide, picking and choosing the best of the swells rolling my way. I like the idea of hitching a ride with a natural force that takes its cues from the circling moon and gathering storm. I relish the thought that my wave has travelled thousands of kilometres and brushed past whales, sharks, and salmon before finishing its journey with me riding its crest. In reality, of course, I wipe out and get tossed around in the foam like a sock in a washing machine.

Long Beach, together with the West Coast Trail and the Broken Group Islands, forms Pacific Rim National Park Reserve. The last few kilometres of the Pacific Rim Highway lead through Long Beach, the accessible heart of the park, and terminate at the government wharf in Tofino.

This is an area of exceptional beaches. There are over 10 kilometres of uninterrupted sandy shore on Long Beach alone, but that is only a fraction of the story. The Long Beach unit of Pacific Rim National Park Reserve also contains Florencia Bay Beach, Wickaninnish Beach, Combers Beach, and the beach at Schooner Cove – in all, 19 kilometres of sandy shore to roam. Just outside the park's northern border are three other gorgeous beaches: the beach at Cox Bay, Chesterman Beach, and MacKenzie Beach. As these beaches are of different sizes, shapes, and angles to the ocean, each has a distinct character and beauty.

Whereas the remote West Coast Trail and the Broken Group Islands are difficult to reach, at Long Beach most of what visitors come to experience is readily accessible – either at the side of the highway or at the end of the road in Clayoquot Sound. It doesn't take a year of physical training or expensive equipment to get out and touch the soul of this place. The eternal surf and the ancient rainforest are both within easy reach.

Noted Canadian naturalist and photographer Janet Foster once said: "The human spirit needs someplace to fly. It needs to know that somewhere it can find sanctuary . . . a place to roam among the spirits of the wilderness." Some find spiritual fulfillment riding an unbroken wave or the wake of a breaching whale. Others find it wandering among the ancient trees or watching the torment of the storm-tossed sea. Whatever it is that makes your spirit fly, Long Beach offers you abundant opportunities to seek and find sanctuary.

Surf City, Canada

Just up the road from Long Beach, behind Tofino's Coffee Pod coffee shop, several surfboards lean against the entrance of Ocean Surf Company. Although it is warm and sunny outside, everyone is inside camped around the television set. Flaked out on futons in the bluish glow are six surfers, photographer Bob Herger, and me. We are watching the latest effort of 22-year-old Allister Fernie — surfer, surf shop manager, and amateur videographer. "Check it out," he says. "Mike's rippin' this one." The television flashes shaky scenes of Adam Smallwood and Mike Stupka sliding up and down 1.5-metre waves at Long Beach. They surf short boards for maximum manoeuvrability and speed.

Allister would rather have been out surfing than holding the camera, but he wasn't able to get in the water because of the new tattoo on his rear end which, incidentally, was also captured in full-colour video. Everyone in the shop has seen it several times, but Allister wants to screen it again for Bob and me. He ejects the surf tape and inserts the tattoo tape. After the video documentary featuring the creation of Allister's latest "body art," he proudly drops his jeans and unveils it live and in person.

These guys surf twice a day. For them, surfing isn't a casual hobby; it is a way of life. But wait a minute. This isn't Southern California, and no one here has a tan. Although surfing has become an established sport on Canada's West Coast, outside of Vancouver Island, Canadian surfing is a well-kept secret. So well-kept, in fact, that at a recent surfing trade show in San Diego, Allister had trouble getting people to take him seriously. "People were constantly underestimating us because we were from Canada," he says. "They have no idea that we surf up here. They thought we'd come to buy surfboards to hang on the wall for decoration!"

Long Beach is Canada's surfing capital. Surfers have been spotted in these waters since the 1960s, and their numbers continue to grow. On any summer Saturday as many as 50 people — men, women, and children alike — can be seen out in the water on short boards, long boards, and body boards.

Originally from Maple Ridge, British Columbia, Allister says he has no plans to return to live on the mainland. "I love to surf and living here lets me go any time I want. It's a good lifestyle. In the city, you look at people and you can tell they don't like what they're doing. Life's too short."

NEXT PAGE: *Smiling on the inside: carving just beyond the curl, Adam Smallwood eyes the glassy road ahead.*

Adam Smallwood, one of the stars of the surfing footage we have just seen, couldn't agree more. He came to Long Beach from Toronto five years ago and hasn't looked back. Adam, 24, started surfing on Lake Ontario and was immediately hooked. "In high school my English essays were about surfing, my history paper was about the first surfers in Polynesia, and I even built a surfboard in art class," he says with an easy grin. "Then I bought a one-way ticket to Vancouver. I showed up at Long Beach with nothing but the clothes on my back. I've been here ever since."

Not the type to do anything in half measures, Adam recalls one of his first days surfing Long Beach. He was in the water for 12 hours straight before passing out from sunstroke. These days Adam has a career in surfing. He works as a surf instructor, as a surfboard repairman, and as a guide for Island Sauvage, a fly-in adventure company that pays him to escort groups out to a secluded beach on Nootka Island for a week of hard-core surfing. It isn't difficult to see that Adam loves his work.

His friend and fellow surfer, Mike Stupka, 20, has curly white hair and looks more the "California Surfer" type, although he probably wouldn't like to hear this. Growing up in Nanaimo, he got addicted to Long Beach at an early age, thanks to numerous family camping trips. "Surfing takes you away from your worries," he explains. "I love dropping in and getting barrelled . . . being out in the ocean as the sun sets. Surfing is a sport that can take you around the world." And it has. Mike has surfed in New Zealand, Australia, Costa Rica, Mexico, and California. Between "surfaris," he regularly returns to Long Beach.

All this surf talk and video footage has them stoked for the real thing. The cast and crew pack up and hit the road in search of waves. At the north end of Long Beach we are greeted with a healthy swell. The waves are glassy and hold their shape. This is the best it has been in weeks, yet the place is practically deserted. Allister and I watch from Incinerator Rock as Mike and Adam, along with three other locals, head out into the waves to put on a show the likes of which I have never seen.

Fast and aggressive, their style is full of steep drops, sharp turns, and endless energy. Mike zips along the top of a wave and then pulls a fast 360-degree turn. Adam somehow gets "tubed" in a scrappy little 1.2-metre wave. Amazing. All the while Allister's videocam is rolling. He narrates a breathless play-by-play that will have the members of the audience back at the surf shop on the edge of their seats. Although he is having fun, watching his friends "rip it up" is like having an itch he just can't scratch. However, it will be a couple more days before he can go out and join them in the water; his brand-new tattoo, a "tribute to Mother Ocean," is still a little on the fresh side.

While hockey may be safe as the national pastime, at Long Beach surfing is the sport of kings — and queens.

NEXT PAGE: *Catching a few z's after a long dance with Mother Ocean.*

Staking a Claim at Florencia Bay

The early morning is fresh, bright blue, and sparkling after the nightlong downpour. I am alone on this exquisite Sunday morning at the start of the Gold Mine Trail. At first the path itself seems unremarkable, and then I see the shafts of God-light beaming through the trees, transforming the mud puddles into pools of mercury. As I make my way down the old logging road, I have two reasons for whistling the same tune over and over: I saw last night's "Bear Necessities" program at Green Point Theatre, and, immediately afterward, I saw a black bear on the road to Kennedy Lake. He got up from his seated position in the middle of the road, ran straight ahead, did a shoulder check, and then lunged into the thick brush. He was fairly big but looked harmless enough from high in the seat of my four-wheel drive. However, now that I am on foot, the odds are definitely in his favour. As I am certainly not interested in sneaking up on him or his friends out here in the forest, I give up on whistling and start singing to the cheap seats.

The signs along the way tell the resource extraction history of the place. They explain that, although the area's first sawmill opened in 1898, full-scale commercial logging didn't begin until 1950. Twenty percent of the park has been logged. This particular stretch leading into Florencia Bay was logged in 1963 and then replanted two years later with Douglas fir and Sitka spruce, two commercially valuable species. Unfortunately neither occurs naturally on this site. The sign assures us that cedar and hemlock will eventually reclaim the forest.

Just before the beach, at Lost Shoe Creek, a sign announces: IN 1899 A UCLUELET INDIAN, TYEE JACK, SPOTTED GOLD IN FLORENCIA BAY. What was found after that first nugget was mostly gold "flour" that had been placer-mined from the cliffs overlooking the beach. The ensuing miniature gold rush didn't really make anyone rich, and the mine was soon abandoned. You can still see bits of old equipment rusting in the grass. Still, if Tyee Jack got lucky, there was at least a lottery-size chance I might find a flake during my morning stroll.

A thin veil of mist rises from the grey, rain-soaked logs as they bake in the summer sun. I look left to Wya Point, I look right to Quisitis Point, and all around I see a little miracle: I am utterly alone in the dazzling sunlight. I walk a few steps farther across

Wya Point and the shores of Florencia Bay.

the untrodden sand and turn to see the imprint of my size-tens trailing behind me. They are the only human footprints on the entire beach. I think of Neil Armstrong. The tide is out and the breakers are gently rolling in, bringing untold discoveries along with them — discoveries that *my* eyes will be the first to see.

There is a totem pole in the grass at the edge of the beach. It is neither Nuu-chah-nulth nor Haida but psychedelic. It was carved to commemorate the birth of a child on the beach back in the summer of 1971, and it is the last reminder of the crowds that once occupied this place. Before the establishment of the park in 1970, there were somewhere in the neighbourhood of 200 squatters living on this beach alone. Some estimate that there were as many as a thousand on the beaches that now make up the Long Beach unit of the park. Some were old-timers who had been in the area for years, but the vast majority were young refugees from the cities in search of a simpler way of life — one unfettered by things like convention, draft boards, and clothes. Others were just looking to get high and have a good time. After being evicted, most left the area, but some settled in Ucluelet and Tofino and have become an integral part of those communities. Others pushed far into Clayoquot Sound and found that simpler life they were looking for.

I comb the shore and find neither shiny lumps of gold nor one of those coveted glass Japanese fishing floats — only kelp, sand dollars, and dried-out crab shells. I have recently learned that these shells aren't the pecked-clean carcasses of dead crabs. Crabs moult as they grow, and these empty shells are just old outer skeletons that have been cast off to make way for expansion.

I stop and stare at Florencia Islet, wading in the middle of the bay. In the winter of 1861, *Florencia,* a Peruvian brig, was wrecked in a cove on the islet after a harrowing 51-day ordeal that saw the loss of its captain and three crew members in a violent gale. The rest were eventually rescued. Today the islet looks placid and inviting. Although I haven't seen the show since I was a kid, Florencia Islet reminds me of *Gilligan's Island.* I sketch it in my notebook.

Eventually, as I start retracing my steps to the trail, it occurs to me that if this beach is public land, then we all have a stake in it. And, since no one else is around, I figure that this is my hour to lay exclusive claim to this strip of our common water-front property. When I leave, I will consider relinquishing title to the next person coming down the trail.

A strip of sand, like a blank page or canvas, is soon filled in with memories and dreams.

From green shoots, carrion, and insects, to wild berries and
salmon, Ursus americanus vancouveri's omnivorous diet is the
key to its survival. When the salmon run out in November, black bears
hibernate until the skunk cabbage sprouts in April. Due to the coast's
temperate climate and lush habitat, coastal black bears have a shorter
denning period than their inland and northern cousins. Black bears are
usually preoccupied with eating, or finding the next meal, so avoid
sneaking up on them by singing, whistling,
or tying bells to your boots.

NEXT PAGE:
Salal and red Indian paintbrush reclaim
driftwood at the rainforest's edge.

Ever-Changing Moods

At Long Beach sunny days are sheer exhilaration. You feel as if you can walk, skip, or run forever. Your spirit soars in this wide-open world, where blues are bluer and greens take on hues you never thought possible. Then, sooner or later, the rain rolls in and washes the colour away.

It rains a lot here. In fact, the west coast of Vancouver Island is the wettest place in Canada. Just how wet, you ask? Long Beach records nearly three metres of precipitation per year. On October 6, 1967, 489.2 millimetres of rain fell on nearby Ucluelet — the greatest rainfall ever recorded on a single day in Canada. The flip side is that this is also the mildest place in Canada, regularly holding the distinction of being the warmest place in the country during the winter.

It didn't take long to notice the difference between myself and the locals when it came to dealing with the rain. I used to run from my vehicle to the restaurant and go through a pot of coffee, waiting for a break in the weather. Eventually I would run back with a newspaper over my head and then drive to my tent and sulk. Along the way, I would notice the locals casually walking from their vehicles to the Co-op, riding around on their bikes, and calmly cleaning fish in the rain. They didn't run around trying to escape the inescapable; they just got wet.

The rain comes in quickly occurring showers that blow in and then out, rolls in as a fine mist, and falls in a constant torrent that can last for days. The dark, dripping forests and monochrome beaches become places of introspection and deeply felt calm. Everything about this wet world feels close and personal.

"Storm-watching" at Long Beach is more than just a marketing scheme to fill hotel rooms in the off-season. For many people the temperamental greys and stormy weather are a real draw. They come during the fall and winter for misty walks on the beach, where the tumultuousness of the surf often achieves epic intensity. They find a feast of fresh salmon or crab, a bottle of wine, and a roaring fire at the end of a dark and blustery day a potent recipe for romance.

A winter morning on Cox Bay.

NEXT PAGE: *The drama of wild winter waves upstages placid Frank Island.*

The area's traditionally rich fish stocks can be reached from charter boats or right off the rocks. For some people the actual catch has little to do with a successful day of fishing.

NEXT PAGE:

As the tide and weather change, so does the landscape. Islands and islets in the mist, like this one at Schooner Cove, become temporarily accessible on foot. When the tide comes in and the sun comes out, such visits seem almost like a dream.

Rainforest Reflections

If, like me, you thought rainforests were steaming, snake-infested jungles in South America or Africa, you are not alone. According to the eighth edition of *Van Nostrand's Scientific Encyclopedia,* a rainforest is "a tropical forest where the annual rainfall is at least 100 inches." It continues as follows: "Several of the world's rainforests have been damaged by anthropogenic activities, and others are severely threatened. Many rainforests are situated in underdeveloped nations that are short of commerce, causing some governments to exploit timber and other assets of the forests as a major means of bettering their economic position."

Digging a little deeper, one discovers that right here in North America we have our own temperate rainforest — the world's largest. It ranges over 3,220 kilometres from the northern tip of the Alaska Panhandle down to San Francisco. It hugs the edge of the Pacific Ocean for the sustaining moisture and mild temperatures that allow it to grow the biggest trees in the world. Pacific Rim National Park Reserve lies right in the heart of this rainforest strip. The park's Spruce Fringe Trail and Rainforest Trail are two of the best places in which to broaden your "rainforest" perspective.

The story begins at the boundary of the windswept sea. Up from Combers Beach the driftwood and eel grass give way to the "spruce fringe" — a thick wind-sheared hedge of stunted spruce, black twinberry, and salmonberry that creates an interlocking barricade against the driving salt spray. It forms a wedge that drives its point toward the beach, being eventually built up with bonsai-shaped trees that grow increasingly larger until finally standing tall and true.

Although the sun is out, inside the spruce fringe it is damp, dark, and primeval. Light penetrates the forest floor in precious few places, but whenever it does, spindly shrubs reach for a sliver of sky. Moss and licorice fern thrive overhead in the boughs of the trees. Crab apple, willows, and a thick growth of salal fill out the forest floor.

Across the highway, the Rainforest Trail leads through virgin stands of amabalis fir, hemlock, and western red cedar, some of which are 800 years old. Safe from the lashing salt spray and unscarred by forest fires, here the towering rainforest reaches its climax. From the leading edge of stunted spruce fringe to the forest of fully realized giants, rain is the driving force behind this vibrant ecosystem.

The skeleton of a salal leaf against the lush green rainforest floor offers a fleeting perspective of the never-ending cycle along the Spruce Fringe Trail.

Aside from the rain, another trait shared by both tropical and temperate rain-forests is that they are disappearing at an unbelievable rate. Governments in "developed" nations are also exploiting the forests for cash. It is estimated that, in the past half century, 50 percent of the world's tropical rainforests and 50 percent of the temperate rainforests have disappeared. Although Clayoquot Sound contains the world's largest remaining areas of unlogged temperate rainforest, on Vancouver Island alone, two-thirds of the old-growth trees are now gone.

More than a quarter of the prescription drugs presently used in Canada come from plant species indigenous to the rainforest. The western yew, found throughout the coastal temperate rainforests, produces taxol, a potential ingredient in the treatment of cancer. No one knows how many other cures for human ills, both physical and spiritual, are vanishing along with the world's shrinking rainforests. A sign posted at the end of the Spruce Fringe Trail begs a moment of sober reflection: "Old-growth forests are more than just old trees, they are intricate, self-renewing ecosystems. As natural forests of old trees are replaced by plantations of young trees, the face of the landscape is changing. Here, the only man-made change is a boardwalk path. While walking along it, we have time to ponder the past and the present. Now it is time to consider the future."

From the leading edge of stunted spruce to the fully realized giants of the Rainforest Trail, rain is the driving force behind this vibrant ecosystem.

NEXT PAGE: *Sanctuary for the human spirit, as well as for the spirits of the wild.*

A moss-covered plank from the original boardwalk trail linking Tofino and Ucluelet recedes into history. Today the Pacific Rim Highway connects the two villages.

People of Salmon and Cedar

In 1778 Captain James Cook sailed into Nootka Sound on his famous voyage of discovery. The Nuu-chah-nulth were there to greet him. They said to him, "*Nootka-a,*" (i.e., "go around") – probably offering directions for navigating the harbour. Cook, thinking they were announcing who they were, called the people and the place in which they lived "Nootka." This classic misunderstanding has been immortalized on maps ever since.

For thousands of years before Cook's arrival, the Nuu-chah-nulth lived well on the bounty of the sea. It is estimated that, prior to European contact, they numbered around 30,000. After contact, smallpox nearly wiped them out. Theirs was a society based on salmon and cedar. Their movements were local and seasonal – in concert with the returning salmon and the ripening berries – and they were accomplished hunters of seals, sea lions, and whales. In winter they worked the cedar. Naturally rot-resistant, cedar was used for canoes and giant communal houses. Cedar bark, which was woven into baskets and clothes, was carefully stripped from living trees – a process that allowed the latter to continue to grow. Today these "culturally modified" trees still stand as a memorial to the intimate relationship between the Nuu-chah-nulth and the forest.

Currently about 200 people of the Tla-o-qui-aht tribe, one of the 14 tribes that make up the Nuu-chah-nulth Tribal Council, live at the north end of Long Beach. They have been living in the area for more than 3,000 years, and Pacific Rim National Park Reserve cannot become an official national park until their land claims are resolved.

Tla-o-qui-aht chief, Francis Frank, is concerned for his people's future. Until recently, fishing and forestry were their main sources of employment, but both of these industries are in sharp decline. This, coupled with the dramatic rise in the number of tourists, has caused a fundamental shift in the Tla-o-qui-aht way of life. "Salmon and cedar are still at the heart of our culture," Chief Frank says. "But things have changed. These days tourism is our main source of industry."

To help capture more of the area's growing tourist market, the tribe has developed Tin Wis Resort, a 56-unit hotel just outside the park. As Chief Frank explains, "The

Carved in 1972 by Nuu-chah-nulth carver Charlie Mickey, this totem pole, located at the Park Information Centre, welcomes visitors to Long Beach and the ancestral home of the Nuu-chah-nulth.

resort allows us to create jobs for ourselves and I think it will let the average tourist become more knowledgeable about First Nations communities — about who and what we are." As the resort continues to develop, he expects to see the addition of more Nuu-chah-nulth culture, including traditional songs and dances, all aimed at increasing understanding. "It's important to help people understand who we are," he says. "But when it comes to putting our culture on display, the elders advise that we must move slow. Our culture is sacred."

A detail from the Park Information Centre totem pole.

Transforming Tofino

I loiter over a steaming cup of coffee and a giant sticky bun at the Common Loaf Bake Shop. The bright interior is filled with the warm, sweet aroma of all things tasty. Next to me a French couple peruses a guidebook. Outside the window, cars go by, with canoes strapped to their roofs. Across the street a mother loads a pickup truck with groceries and kids as men in mack jackets walk down the road to work. I finish my coffee and join the morning rush.

Located in a privileged position between Long Beach and Clayoquot Sound, Tofino has gone through enormous growing pains over the past decade in its transition from isolated fishing village, to commercial logging centre, to eco-tourist Mecca. A tide of more than 300,000 visitors washes over Tofino every summer and, when it recedes, it leaves behind the 1,300 people who call the place home.

Lisa Mulder is one person who will still be here when the high season is over. Although she keeps a desk at Interfor — the small forest-green building on the way into town — she can be a difficult person to track down. A silviculturist, she is often out at logging sites or busy growing trees.

One of only three female foresters on the west coast of Vancouver Island, Lisa is used to being outnumbered. Although she often finds it challenging and frustrating to establish herself in a male-dominated field, she assures me it is well worth the effort. "You have to be tough," she says. "But I love it. The job appeals to me because it's ecology and biology. It's important. I get a lot of time in helicopters and floatplanes so I know the sound like the back of my hand. Every day I do something different."

Lisa moved to Tofino in 1994 and, although working in forestry can be a constant challenge for a woman, she says that getting accepted in town was not: "It's so welcoming. Tofino is the most dynamic and open town I've ever lived in — and I've lived in a lot of small communities." Lisa is no stranger to the political debate surrounding her work. In a way, the community of Tofino itself is now defined by the debate between those committed to stopping what they see as the destruction of the rainforests and those who support the logging industry. Even attempting to define the debate is a political process. "People here are very steadfast in what they believe," Lisa says. "As a forester, I know that we have more standards to live up to. We're working hard to meet

A village on the edge: traditional resource extraction industries such
as commercial fishing and logging are being eclipsed by
tourism, recreation, and sport fishing.

those standards and to log in a way that minimizes the impact on the public and the environment. We want to be a part of the community. We don't want to walk away and leave what we've started."

In Tofino people live their lives close to the wilderness. And because most of them depend on it for their income, either in terms of resource extraction or tourism, they hold passionate opinions about how it should or should not be used. Dorothy Baert, for example, owner of Tofino Sea Kayaking, has an opinion about logging in Clayoquot Sound. Her business depends on the wild, natural beauty of the lush mountains, quiet coves, and clean beaches. Her livelihood comes from catering to the growing number of paddlers looking for a pristine wilderness adventure. What these people don't want to see, she says, are clearcuts.

Opened in 1988, Tofino Sea Kayaking now has 33 rental boats and serves thousands of paddlers each season by providing guided tours, rentals, a kayak school, and the Paddler's Inn bed-and-breakfast. "The first big rush came in 1989 when *Outside* magazine featured Tofino as one of their top ten places to visit," Dorothy says. "Then after the Clayoquot Sound protests in 1993, things really accelerated. What people love is paddling itself. They're paddling their own craft, and that control brings a kind of intimacy. You're moving at your own pace and perspective. You can see a physical change in people when they come back from a trip — from their posture to their facial expression. It makes them feel connected."

Just up the road from Tofino Sea Kayaking, the Co-op grocery store on the corner of First and Campbell stands at the crossroads of the community. Everyone ends up there at least once or twice a week — fishers, loggers, environmentalists, and tourists alike. What is it like to share a small village with people of such differing opinions? "It can be hard on a daily basis but people are generally quite gracious," Dorothy explains. "It's also very rewarding. If you have a disagreement, usually you get to come away respectful of the person. The well-being of the community comes first. We keep things open and in discussion."

Ken Gibson is one of those people who is eager to discuss the community's past, present, and future. Born and raised in Tofino, Ken spent a lifetime working in settlements all up and down the coast, building wharves and marinas. "I was born in 1935 in a trading post down near the dock," he says. "I've lived in Tofino all my life. I couldn't find any place I like better." And the rain? "I don't mind it. We're the salmon people, you know. We can't deal with the extreme heat or cold."

One of the early proponents of a park at Long Beach, Ken, like many Tofino residents, has been amazed by the increase in tourism. And while some people are concerned about the pace of development, he thinks it is just what the area needs. "It's a clean industry," he says. "I can't see anything wrong with it. They bring in new money and don't leave anything behind."

Tourists do, however, bring surprises. "One thing us old-timers never imagined was that people would pay $65 each to go out and see a bunch of whales," Ken says.

A curious crab has an out-of-water experience near Meares Island.
It doesn't get any fresher than this.

"Things have *really* changed. During World War II, they trained fliers here. Tofino was the third largest air base in Canada. They used bald eagles for target practice, they practised bombing runs on grey whales, and the small fighter aircraft strafed Sea Lion Rocks. Now our jobs depend on the wildlife."

In addition to Tofino's main draws – wildlife, scenery, and solitude – another popular attraction is art. One former resident who has left an indelible mark on the community is internationally acclaimed First Nations artist Roy Henry Vickers. His prominent Eagle Aerie Gallery is the most visited attraction in town. Created in the tradition of a First Nations longhouse, the gallery shelters most of Roy's original works and welcomes over 300,000 visitors a year. His serigraphs and paintings, hanging on the cedar-plank walls, are evocative images that blend traditional Northwest Coast aboriginal forms with a modern graphic style. Many people make the trip to Tofino just to visit this gallery.

"I knew that if I built the building of my dreams here it would succeed," Roy says. "It wasn't a risk. The dream came true even larger than I could have envisioned." After living in Tofino for 15 years, Roy now divides his time between his new home and gallery in the Victoria area, his original Tofino gallery, and an itinerary that literally takes him around the world. Roy, who worked as a commercial fisherman when he first came to Tofino in 1980, has seen his life, and that of the community, take off in a whole new direction.

"The world is changing and Tofino is changing," he says. "If you keep extracting the natural resources, eventually you won't have anything left. But if you look after the land, people will come to see it. In creating that gallery, people saw that if you build something beautiful – not a row of neon lights and tourist traps, but showed your love for the land – you can make this place beautiful. It can be done. And they have."

"They're paddling their own craft," says Dorothy Baert of Tofino
Sea Kayaking, "and that control brings a kind of intimacy. . . .
You can see a physical change in people when they
come back from a trip – from their posture to
their facial expression. It makes
them feel connected."

NEXT PAGE: *The view of Tofino harbour to*
Opitsat and Meares Island.

Striking out with compass and chart, paddlers from all over the world take to the rich waters of Clayoquot Sound each summer. With secluded coves and pristine beaches, Clayoquot is big and wild enough to accommodate a large number of people-powered pleasure craft.

NEXT PAGE
As a female California sea lion looks on, cormorants and a seagull vie for prime real estate on Plover Reef in Clayoquot Sound.

MEARES ISLAND

Sentinel of the Sound

Deep green and grey, Meares Island looms over Tofino like an omen. Its twin peaks, Mount Colnett and Lone Cone, dominate the viewscape to the north and east of the village and can be seen all the way from the park. Its trees, identifiable individuals, crowd the steep slopes across the waters of Browning Passage. The inescapable presence of Meares Island, as much as the sea itself, defines the area and offers a preview of the lush, rich environment that is Clayoquot Sound.

I am the only passenger on this small boat. On the short trip across, my skipper recounts the trials and fortunes of the past tourist season — the increasing numbers of people and the growing competition in the water taxi business conducted between Tofino and Meares. People keep coming to see the trees that stand at the centre of one of the hottest environmental campaigns in Canadian history. They come to see what all the fuss is about.

When we land on the rock that starts the Big Tree Trail, I can see the wooden boardwalk winding into the dense forest. I have the place to myself. The murmur of the boat fades into the afternoon as I enter the woods. I walk along the trail for a few moments, then stop. Sunlight filters through the tall canopy. It makes its way through the branches, lichen, and ferns to my open notebook. It warms the back of my hand.

A sign tips me off to an eagle's nest high in a weathered old cedar. I wonder how many of these majestic raptors make their home on the island's 8,800 hectares. Seeing no movement, I continue on. It isn't long, however, until I hear the weak, high-pitched twittering of a bald eagle. I smile as I remember the park interpreter explaining that the bald eagle's call isn't macho enough for American television. When a bald eagle is used in commercials down south, they remove its natural, wimpy call and dub in the fierce cry of the red-tailed hawk instead.

I arrive at the Hanging Garden Tree, a gnarled giant that measures 18.3 metres in circumference. It is the largest known living cedar in Canada. Some say it is more than 1,500 years old. In fact, it is so large and has been around for so long that it seems to have become its own ecosystem. From its upper branches to its lower trunk, life abounds. Licorice and sword ferns, mosses, lichens, salal bushes, and even smaller hemlock trees grow out of snags in the side of its trunk, forming "hanging gardens" — miniature islands in the air.

Hanging Garden Tree on Meares Island: so large and ancient it seems to have become its own ecosystem.

Meares is famous as the home of some of the largest cedar, spruce, and hemlock trees in the world. Some of these trees grow to heights in excess of 60 metres. Ninety-five percent of the island's rainforest is old-growth and still looks as it did when European eyes first saw it more than two centuries ago.

In the mid-1980s, protesters, representing a broad coalition of Tofino residents, First Nations, and environmentalists, drew a line of demarcation around the shore of Meares Island. Some were worried that logging the island would mar their view, others were concerned with the integrity of their water supply, but most were bent on preserving the vanishing old-growth temperate rainforest. The protests caught the imagination of the province, and the issue spilled over into the international media.

In 1984 the Tla-o-qui-aht declared a "tribal park" on their ancestral island. Eventually a court injunction stopped the logging, but the issue is still not resolved. A decade after the beginning of the moratorium on logging on Meares Island, the government still hasn't recognized the tribal park, and the island is still not officially protected. Nothing much is expected to happen until treaty negotiations take place. Until then, and long after, the island's protectors will be vigilant.

A bald eagle keeps a watchful eye over the tribal park on Meares Island. Don't be fooled by the wimpy voice.

NEXT PAGE: *Wandering among the ankles of the giants on Meares Island's Big Tree Trail.*

A Clayoquot Discovery

Three of us wait on Fisherman's Wharf. The place is deserted. It is five to nine in the morning, and I *think* this is the rendezvous point for our water taxi, but I am not sure. My old friends Brian Beaulac, a Seattle hotelier, and Mark Robinson, a Ladner high school teacher, look to me for answers. We check the names of the boats tied up along the dock. No joy. Then, simultaneously, we see and hear the *Matlaha Pride* come cruising around Stubbs Island. It is right on time.

Clifford Lucas, a member of the Hesquiat tribe from Hot Springs Cove, tells us the journey will take a little over an hour. Inside the sturdy aluminum boat are rows of red seats — much like those one might find in a small school bus. We stand outside on the aft deck and watch Tofino harbour quickly slip away. We pass fishing charters, weather-worn houseboats, and groups of kayakers camped on a white sandy beach. The moment we pass the relative protection of Vargas Island, the sea tosses up 1.5-metre swells. The bow slices through the hills and plunges down the valleys with speed and purpose. We hold a course toward our destination on the far side of Clayoquot Sound.

CLOSE ENCOUNTERS

About 15 minutes into the voyage, Clifford suddenly stops, brings the boat around, and points down into the water. We squint into the darkening depths. "I thought it was a whale," he announces. "It's not. Looks like a sunfish."

The ghostly grey figure hovering below the surface doesn't look like any fish we have ever seen. About three metres across, it is round and flat with two giant fins and looks like an escapee from another epoch. We resume our northwesterly course and our search for cetacean life. Five minutes later Clifford spots the spray of a sounding grey whale.

Again our skipper slows the engine and executes a sharp turn toward the open sea. I feel compelled to point out the obvious, that we seem to be on a collision course with the thing, but I keep quiet and ready my camera. "Watch the spray," he says. "It'll come up somewhere in front." Sure enough, the barnacle-encrusted back of a grey

Early-morning sun dries the rain from the boughs of a western hemlock on Vargas Island.

whale, spotted white on smooth grey skin, rises out of the water. Its exhale and inhale are loud and deep.

Clifford cuts the engine. We quietly ride the swell, waiting until the whale comes up not more that four metres off our port side. I rapidly shoot off three or four frames, hoping we won't get tossed into the drink. Brian stares speechless, and Mark mumbles, "It's as big as the boat." Then it is gone in a flourish of bubbles and wake. Again it emerges headfirst, lets fly that fast exchange of old air for new, arches its back, and waves its tail in the air before the descent. We fire up the engines and follow it back the way we came.

We are getting more than we bargained for with this trip. Although this is a water taxi, not a whale-watching tour, Clifford seems more than willing to indulge in a diversion. He gets on the radio and announces the location and direction of our discovery. A whale-watching tour approaches from the south to take over the vigil. Finally we turn around and resume our original course.

Whales are one of the main draws for visitors to Tofino and Clayoquot Sound. Last year 45,000 people took whale-watching excursions from Tofino. In terms of ticket sales and direct employment — plus spin-off benefits to hotels, restaurants, and shops — it is estimated that the new "whaling industry" adds nearly $10 million to the local economy annually.

Grey whales, a baleen whale species, can reach lengths of 13.5 metres. Once hunted to the edge of extinction, they now return to the protected waters of Clayoquot Sound on a yearly migration that takes them from summer feeding grounds in Alaska to winter breeding grounds off Mexico's Baja Peninsula. Between 30 and 50 greys return to Clayoquot Sound each year. Some individuals have been calling into the area for over 20 years. Tofino and Ucluelet celebrate the event in March with the annual Pacific Rim Whale Festival.

Unlike the relatively common greys, orcas — or killer whales — are seen less frequently in local waters. With slick black and white skin, tall dorsal fins, and blunt white teeth, orcas are the largest members of the dolphin family. Although orcas have been spotted in Clayoquot Sound in every month of the year, July and August offer the best chance for a sighting.

The other whale that was once common in local waters is the humpback. Once an important source of food for the Nuu-chah-nulth, humpbacks were hunted from dugout canoes. The hunt itself was an event steeped in ritual and reverence. It is said that the coveted position of harpoonist always went to the chief, who was limited to taking only 10 whales in his lifetime. Early Europeans arrived with a different idea about whale quotas and, in short order, very nearly liquidated the entire species. The recent sighting of a lone humpback in the area is a hopeful sign that these whales may one day return to Clayoquot Sound.

In the longest migration of any mammal, grey whales travel up to 15,000 kilometres annually. En route, between 30 and 50 greys pass through Clayoquot Sound.

NEXT PAGE: *Orca (or killer whale) pods fall into three groups: resident, which live in the same area year-round; transient, which travel up and down the coast; and offshore. Offshore pods have only recently been identified and little is known of their behaviour. This pair, spotted off Flores Island, are from a transient pod.*

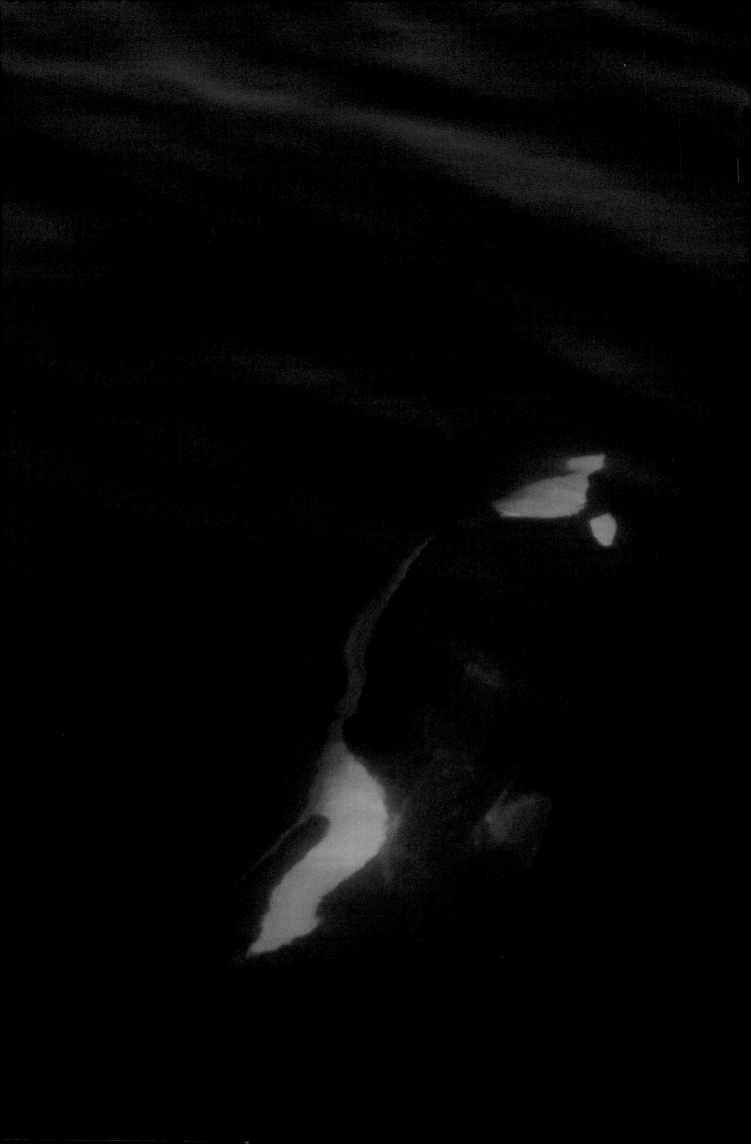

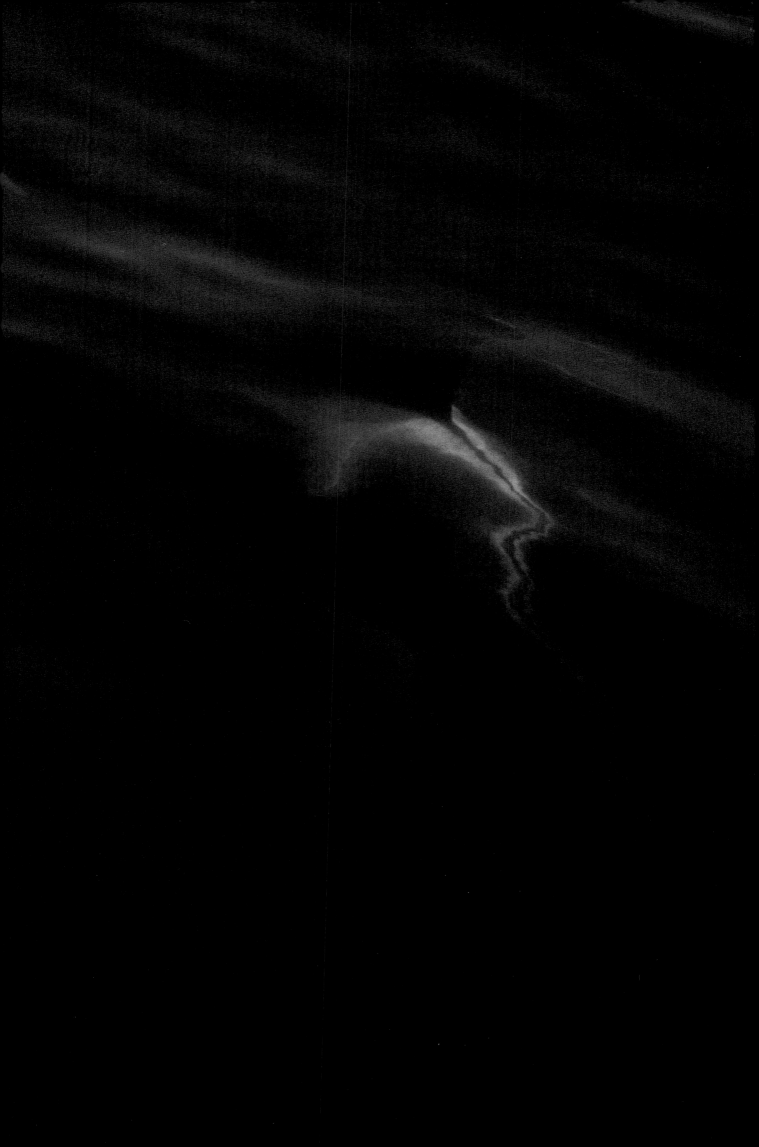

Another endangered species, the temperate rainforest, fills the view off our starboard side. Old-growth, patched with sections of young second-growth, cover the hills and mountains. Recent landslides — most of which are in areas that were once clearcut — scar the otherwise uninterrupted green.

Over the roar of the engine, Mark, Brian, and I discuss the summer of 1993 and the highly publicized protests to stop clearcutting in Clayoquot Sound. Ten thousand people from all walks of life came here to halt the rapid loss of old-growth. They succeeded in slowing the pace of logging in Clayoquot Sound. The confrontation also led to the Interim Measures Agreement, which resulted in (1) First Nations being given an equal voice with the provincial government with regard to making decisions that would affect the forest; (2) the creation of a scientific panel to set new forest management standards; and (3) worldwide media attention which, in turn, resulted in a fresh wave of eco-tourists.

The *Matlaha Pride* takes us close to the shore of Flores Island, past rocky headlands, moss-covered giant hemlock, and grey cedar snags. Before the Clayoquot protests, most Canadians didn't even know they had a rainforest. Then, suddenly, the world was watching and the pressure was on to save it. It took the largest protest in Canadian history, the arrest of 932 people, and the largest mass trial in the Western world to do it. As with the humpback whale, so with the rainforest: we are getting another chance to turn things around. And, if public response over the past decade is any indication, there is reason to hope we can be successful.

The voyage is coming to an end. As we approach the Sharp Point lighthouse on the tip of Openit Peninsula, not far from the hot springs, I ask Clifford about wild winter storms and dangerous seas. On the way into the sheltered cove, he tells me that there were only three times last year when he couldn't make the daily run from Hot Springs Cove to Tofino. "On one of those days," he says in a matter-of-fact tone, "I saw a wave as tall as that lighthouse." I check later and find out that the lighthouse is 18 metres high.

SPRINGS ETERNAL

David Letson, owner and caretaker of the new camping area near the trailhead to the hot springs, takes a hands-on approach to his place. With short grey hair, smiling eyes, and a well-worn Hot Springs Cove T-shirt, he invites us to choose a spot. He has christened each campsite with individual names, like "Creekside" and "Salal." We choose "Old Hemlock," which has an excellent view of the village across the cove. It is also next to a very handy covered cooking area, Dave's shed, and the firewood he has collected and split for campers. He has even made little cedar stools for each site. The place has "retirement project" written all over it.

Low tide reveals a jackpot of sand dollars in a lucky wishbone array.

The well-maintained boardwalk to the hot springs at Maquinna Provincial Park is itself a landmark. Many of the planks on the trail bear the names of crew members who came ashore to warm their bones. Some are simple, unembellished markers carved into the existing cedar planks, while others are more elaborate creations with inlaid rope and varnish.

At the end of the half-hour trail the smell of sulphur is strong. It is "Mak-seh-kla-chuck," or "smoking waters," as the Nuu-chah-nulth call it. The source is near the top of a hill, where the water bubbles to the surface at 50 degrees Celsius. It cascades down in a steaming stream, showers over a little cliff, then tumbles into a miniature canyon of pools before finally reaching the sea. We start at the hot shower, work our way down the gradually cooling pools, and then back again.

As the tide comes in, it washes over the rocks and floods the lower pools. We hold on to a big boulder and let the cool water race over our backs as the fresh water warms our bellies. A few people take the seaweed that has just washed in and drape it around their necks and over their heads. A German couple dive into the surf at the end of the spring. Mark, Brian, and I dive in behind them. It isn't long before the bracing cold sends us scrambling back up the rocks to the hot shower at the top of the little canyon.

We spend the afternoon in a changing group of bathers. Eventually everyone gets acquainted while being sloshed around in the tide-washed tubs. We meet a fisherman from Ahousat, a couple from Seattle, a woman from New York, and an off-duty park naturalist from Long Beach. There are never more than 10 of us at a time. The little canyon isn't a roomy place, and I can't imagine it comfortably holding many more. However, back at camp, Dave Letson tells us that he has seen up to 45 people at a time trying to stick their toes into the steaming water. In winter, he adds, the place is often deserted.

After dinner and a fire on the beach back at "Old Hemlock," we decide to make a second trip over the boardwalk trail to the hot springs. Dusk is past and we navigate the path by the dim starlight. We arrive at the empty pools, peel down to our birthday suits, and soak up the warmth. Shortly afterward, other people start to appear. They disrobe and slide in. Unlike the afternoon, when people wore trunks and bikinis, this evening everyone is au naturel. We take turns going from the hot pools to the cooling ocean.

Our fellow bathers are from the yachts moored out in the cove. A couple on a round-the-world voyage talks quietly at first, but soon the conversation grows until it takes everyone away to foreign ports and southern seas. The bubbling spring and the pounding surf provide the sound track. The candles, flickering along the rock walls, cast the bathers in a warm golden light. It all transports us fortunate few to a state of primal relaxation.

Tomorrow we will all leave Clayoquot Sound. Our new companions will be sailing up the coast, and we will return to Tofino. But in this close, secluded place, as we soak in water fresh from the earth, all thoughts of tomorrow wash away. They trickle down the shiny black rocks and out into the surf, leaving only the moment behind.

Bathing in primitive luxury at "Mak-seh-kla-chuck," or "smoking waters."

Last Stop, Ucluelet

My kid sister stands outside in the mud. Our tent and most of its contents are soaked. Thankfully the morning sky brightens and the sun promises to poke through the mist.

Elizabeth, 16, is up from the United States for a short holiday, and despite three consecutive days of rainforest conditions, I remain determined to show her a good time. She isn't complaining, but she has that slightly blasé teenage disposition, just as I had when I was her age. We will see what we can do about that.

At the north end of Long Beach we dress in black neoprene. The waves are small, perfect for learning. After demonstrating how to wax a board and where to strap a leash, I take five minutes and tell her everything I know about surfing. Then I snap a few pictures for the folks back home.

Although she gasps when the first wave splashes over her head, she is delighted to find that I am telling the truth; it only takes a few minutes before everything starts warming up. I tell her to forget trying to stand her first time out. She should start with body boarding to get a feel for the workings of a wave. I keep offering pointers and encouragement until she politely tells me to lay off and let her do it on her own. I paddle out past the break.

After half an hour of watching waves either pass her by or push her off her board, I wonder if she is starting to get frustrated. Finally she catches a ride. I shout, "Yes!" and then get smacked in the back of the head by an incoming wave. But I regain my composure in time to see her take it all the way to the sand. When she gets up and turns around, a smile stretches wide cross her face. She can't hide her excitement.

Too soon it is time to go. As we leave the parking lot, I notice the fuel light flashing on the dashboard. I have learned over the years that if you don't fill up on food and gas before leaving the coast, it is a long 100 kilometres before you get a second chance. We drive south to Ucluelet.

This afternoon the streets of the village are nearly deserted. We pass by the *Canadian Princess*, a historic 70-metre steamship permanently moored in the harbour. A floating hotel, it has staterooms for 80 guests and is the flagship of Ucluelet's tourism industry. In a few weeks it will close for the season.

Ucluelet and Tofino stand at opposite ends of Long Beach. Although similar in

Reading the waves: in surfing, as in life, timing is everything.

size and proximity to the park, Ucluelet has a more modest reputation as a tourist destination. Primarily a commercial fishing and logging community, Ucluelet is also a launching point for whale-watching and sport-fishing excursions to Barkley Sound and the Broken Group Islands. As jobs in traditional resource industries become more scarce, there is little doubt Ucluelet will vie for a larger share of the region's growing tourism market.

We find a decidedly untrendy coffee shop. I suspect the wood panelling and Formica interior hasn't changed much since the 1950s. The waitress is familiar with almost everyone in the place, and by the way patrons are socializing, I imagine we are the token tourists. The menu, noticeably light on nouvelle cuisine and vegetarian options, is just what the doctor ordered. We fill up on cheeseburgers.

Night falls as we make our way across the island, and Elizabeth keeps me awake with her plans to attend the University of Victoria. As she talks of campus housing and tuition fees, my mind wanders back a dozen years or so to that corner of the sports equipment room at the university. I wonder if she will stroll in there one day and find that same old relic of a surfboard. If she does, at least she will know how to use it.

Finally I venture the question, "So. Long Beach. What did you think?"

"It was fun," she replies through a yawn. "No one's going to believe I went surfing in Canada."

It will be a few weeks before Elizabeth's card arrives sandwiched between the credit card bill and the junk mail. In it she will say, with uncharacteristic enthusiasm, that riding the waves at Long Beach was "one of the greatest times of my life."

Summer is over. Soon I will get caught up in the rising tide of work, and before I know it, I will be singing Christmas carols. But for now I am content. My face is red and my shoulders ache. My camera is full of memories, and everywhere there is sand.

Surfers follow the swell. When it's flat at Long Beach, it might be crankin' at Cox Bay. Being adaptable means you can take advantage of a good thing while it lasts. Because before you know it, conditions change.

NEXT PAGE: *Ucluelet has become a launching point for whale-watching and sport-fishing excursions, as these boats in the village's harbour testify.*

If You Go

Pacific Rim National Park Reserve

The Park Information Centre is open from mid-March to October and is located near the park's entrance on Pacific Rim Highway. It is a one-stop source for park orientation, guidebooks, and a schedule of guided hikes and events. Open 9:30 a.m. to 5:00 p.m. Phone: (250) 726-4212.

Wickaninnish Centre, the park's major visitor centre, offers theatre programs, exhibits, displays, and group activities to help visitors learn about the park's marine ecology, ocean, and rainforest environment. Licensed restaurant. Located on Wickaninnish Beach. Open 10:30 a.m. to 6:00 p.m. daily mid-March to mid-October. Phone: (250) 726-7333.

The park has 94 drive-in camping sites and 54 walk-in sites at Green Point. There are no hookups or sani-stations. Maximum stay is seven days. Phone: (800) 689-9025 for rates, reservations, and information. During the summer, Green Point Theatre offers excellent interpretive evening programs that are both informative and entertaining. Admission is free for campers registered at Green Point Campground, $2 for noncampers.

TRANSPORTATION

Long Beach and Tofino are six hours from Vancouver, five hours from Victoria, and three hours from Nanaimo. For transportation information, contact:
ISLAND COACH LINES: (250) 724-1266
NORTH VANCOUVER AIR: (800) 228-6608
TOFINO AIRLINES: (250) 725-4454
B.C. FERRIES: (604) 669-1211
WASHINGTON STATE FERRY INFORMATION: (206) 464-6400.

Tofino

The Tofino Tourism Information Centre is the best place to find current prices and a list of companies offering whale-watching excursions, kayak rental, and fishing charters to Meares Island and Hot Springs Cove; scuba diving; flight-seeing; and information on camping, hotels, resorts, bed-and-breakfasts, and schedules of events. Open early spring through fall, seven days a week, in peak season. Address: Box 249, 346 Campbell Street, Tofino, B.C. VOR 2Z0. Phone: (250) 725-3414.

ACCOMMODATION

The following list includes resorts, hotels, motels, and cottages. For information on bed-and-breakfasts, contact the Tofino Tourism Information Centre at (250) 725-3414.

CABLE COVE INN: Waterfront view. Private Jacuzzi baths, fireplaces, and hot tub. Walking distance from town. (800) 663-6449; (250) 725-4236. Box 339, 201 Main Street.

CRYSTAL COVE BEACH RESORT AND CAMPGROUND: Oceanfront log cottages, one- and two-bedrooms, kitchens, fireplaces or wood stoves. 12 units. (250) 725-4213. Box 559, 1165 Cedarwood Place.

DOLPHIN MOTEL: Three kilometres south of Tofino, near to beach. Housekeeping or sleeping units with kitchen access. Combination baths. Pets okay. 13 units. (250) 725-3377. Box 116, 1190 Pacific Rim Highway.

DUFFIN COVE RESORT MOTEL: Scenic waterfront units, close to village. Cabins with fireplaces, kitchenettes, private balconies, and queen beds; will sleep six. 13 units. (250) 725-3448. Box 178, 215 Campbell Street.

HIMWITSA LODGE: Scenic Tofino waterfront. Queen beds, combination baths, kitchens, TV, VCR, hot tub. Four units. (800) 665-9425; (250) 725-2017. Box 176, 300 Main Street.

MACKENZIE BEACH RESORT: Individual beach-front cottages two kilometres south of Tofino. Heated pool/spa. Full kitchens, fireplaces. No pets. 14 units. Campground available. (250) 725-3439. Box 12, 1101 Pacific Rim Highway.

MIDDLE BEACH LODGE: On secluded beach two kilometres south of Tofino. Queen beds, lounge with fireplace. 26 units. Breakfast included. (250) 725-2900. Box 413, 400 MacKenzie Beach Road.

MINI MOTEL: A-frames in gardens on Tofino Inlet. TV, kitchens, sleeping units with view decks and barbecues. Five units. (250) 725-3441. Box 26, 350 Olsen Road.

OCEAN VILLAGE BEACH RESORT: Three kilometres south of Tofino. Cottages on MacKenzie Beach with ocean views, kitchens, queen beds, heated indoor pool, and whirlpool. 51 units. (250) 725-3755. Box 490, 555 Hellesen Drive.

ORCA LODGE: Three kilometres south of Tofino. Double beds, hide-a-beds, combination baths, TV, fine dining, licensed lounge, complimentary Continental breakfast. (250) 725-2323. Box 246, 1254 Pacific Rim Highway.

PACIFIC SANDS BEACH RESORT: Housekeeping cottages and suites on Cox Bay Beach with kitchens and fireplaces. Some hot tubs, no pets. Seven kilometres south of Tofino. (800) 565-2322; (250) 725-3322. Box 237, 1421 Pacific Rim Highway.

SCHOONER MOTEL: Central location with Tofino Inlet and mountain views. 16 suites and sleeping units, cable, no pets. Double and queen beds, some kitchens. (250) 725-3478. Box 202, 311 Campbell Street.

TIN WIS BEST WESTERN: Beachfront resort, licensed restaurant, beach access, cable, no pets, combination baths, direct-dial phones, gift shop. 56 units. (800) 661-9995; (250) 725-4445. Box 389, 1119 Pacific Coast Highway.

TOFINO SWELL LODGE: Seven waterfront units overlooking Meares Island. Twin, queen, and king units, private baths, large shared kitchen, outdoor hot tub, barbecue area, boat charters, and moorage. (250) 725-3274. Box 160, 341 Olsen Road.

WEIGH WEST MARINE RESORT: On Tofino harbour, sleeping units or kitchen suites. Charters, guest moorage, restaurant, and pub. 63 units. (800) 665-8922; (250) 725-3277. Box 69, 634 Campbell Street.

WICKANINNISH INN AND POINTE RESORT: On a rocky promontory overlooking Chesterman Beach. Nonsmoking. 46 guest rooms, restaurant, conference, and banquet facilities. (800) 333-4604; (250) 725-3100. Box 250, Osprey at Chesterman Beach.

CAMPING

BELLA PACIFICA: 143 oceanfront and wilderness sites, beach and nature trails. Full hookups, flush toilets, and free showers. Reservations accepted. (250) 725-3400. Box 413, 400 MacKenzie Beach.

MAQUINNA PROVINCIAL PARK: Located at Hot Springs Cove, 40 kilometres north of Tofino by boat or plane.

MACKENZIE BEACH RESORT: See Accommodation listing above.

RECREATION

LIVE TO SURF: Surfboards, body boards, and wet suit rentals. (250) 725-4464. 1180 Pacific Rim Highway.

OCEAN SURF: Surfboards, body boards, and wet suit sales and rentals. Surf lessons and information. (250) 725-3344. 171 Fourth Street.

PACIFIC KAYAK CENTRE: Adventure cove tours, sunset trips, Meares Island trips, and kayak rentals. (250) 725-3232. General Delivery, 564B Campbell Street.

RAINCOAST COMMUNICATIONS: Naturalist-led tours exploring the wilderness and cultural history of the West Coast. Call for updates of weekly events. (250) 725-2878. Box 386, Tofino, B.C.

REMOTE PASSAGES: Sea kayaking day trips — guided only. Interpretive programs — no experience necessary. (800) 666-9833; (250) 725-3330/3380. Box 624, Meares Landing at 71 Wharf Street.

TOFINO SEA KAYAKING: Single and multiday nature tours. Lodge-based and wilderness camping. No experience required. Rentals, courses, supplies, and information. (800) TOFINO-4; (250) 725-4222. Box 620, 320 Main Street.

Undersea Dive Charters: Tanks, dive gear, and guides. (250) 725-2755. Box 540, 596 Pfeiffer Crescent.

CHARTERS

Chinook Charters: Whale-watching excursions, Hot Springs Cove tours and fishing charters by local guides. (800) 665-3646; (250) 725-3431. Box 501, 450 Campbell Street.

Clayoquot Whaler: Whale-watching, nature/eco tours aboard 9.6-metre aluminum boat. Departing three times daily from Fourth Street Wharf. (888) 49-whale; (250) 725-3195. 411 Campbell Street.

Cypre Prince Tours: Springtime whale-watching. Specializing in summer fishing charters, jig boat. Will combine groups. (800) 787-2202; (250) 725-2202. Box 149, 430 Campbell Street.

Jamie's Whaling Station: Tofino's original whale watch — guaranteed sightings. Hot Springs Cove and fishing charters. Bed-and-breakfast accommodation available. (800) 667-9913 (B.C. & Alberta); (250) 725-3919. Box 590, 606 Campbell Street.

R&S Tours at Weigh West Marine Resort: Interpretive whale cruises, custom nature tours, and fishing charters in a seven-metre Boston Whaler. (250) 725-3277/3958. Box 213, 634 Campbell Street.

Remote Passages: Whale-watching, Hot Springs Cove, nature observation, personalized education programs. Zodiac specialists. (800) 666-9833; (250) 725-3330. Box 624, Meares Landing at 71 Wharf Street.

Sea-Trek Tours and Expeditions: Whale-watching, Hot Springs Cove, harbour and nature tours, Meares Island, hiking, camping, and fishing. English, French, and German tours. (250) 725-4412. Box 627, 441B Campbell Street.

Seaforth Charters: Sport-fishing charters, whale-watching, and sightseeing. (250) 725-4252. Box 217, 448 Campbell Street.

Springtime Charters: Year-round sport fishing, 25 years experience. All-inclusive tours in 6.3-metre Custom Cruiser. Freshwater steelhead fishing available. (250) 725-2351. Box 608, Tofino, B.C.

Whale Centre and Museum, Nature Watch Excursions Ltd.: Whale-watching, Meares Island, black bear observations, Hot Springs excursions, and 8.4-metre covered boat and five-metre Boston Whaler. (250) 725-2132. Box 393, 411 Campbell Street.

Weigh West Fishing Charters: Fully guided, 6.3- to 7-metre Wellcrafts. Packages available. (800) 665-8922. Box 69, 634 Campbell Street.

GALLERIES

Eagle Aerie Gallery: Featuring works of Roy Henry Vickers. Original limited-edition paintings and carvings in a Northwest Coast First Nations-style longhouse gallery. (800) 663-0669; (250) 725-3235. Box 10, 350 Campbell Street.

House of Himwitsa: Native art gallery featuring limited-edition prints, jewellery, totems, carvings, and pottery in a dynamic setting. (800) 665-9425; (250) 725-2017. Box 176, 300 Main Street.

Rainforest Gallery: Over 95 artists, both Native and non-Native, are represented in this large gallery located over the Schooner Restaurant. (250) 725-2194. Box 464, 331 Campbell Street.

EMERGENCY SERVICES

Police / Fire / Ambulance: 911.
Police (nonemergency calls): (250) 725-3242.
Hospital (Tofino General): (250) 725-3212.
261 Neill Street, Tofino.

Ucluelet

The Ucluelet Chamber of Commerce InfoCentre is the best place to find current prices and a list of companies offering whale-watching, kayak rental, fishing charters, and excursions as well as information on camping, hotels, resorts, bed-and-breakfasts, and schedules of events. Open year-round, seven days a week in peak season, five days a week off-season. Address: Box 428, 227 Main Street, Ucluelet, B.C. V0R 3A0. Phone: (250) 726-4641.

ACCOMMODATION

The following list includes hotels, motels, and cottages. For information on bed-and-breakfasts, contact the Ucluelet Chamber of Commerce InfoCentre.

BRENDA'S PLACE: Kitchen, private bath, sleeps five. (250) 726-7107. Box 614, 362 Yew Street.

CANADIAN PRINCESS RESORT: Historic ship permanently moored in Ucluelet harbour. Lounge, dining rooms, and shore units with fireplaces. (800) 663-7090; (250) 726-7771. Box 939, 1943 Peninsula Road.

4 CEDARS COTTAGE: Self-contained, private cottage overlooking the harbour. Close to walking trails. (250) 726-4284. Box 458, 1183 Eber Road.

CEDAR COTTAGES: Cabins located on Ucluelet Island with full kitchen, living room, and one bedroom. (250) 726-4402. Box 855, 2465 Pacific Rim Highway.

ISLAND WEST RESORT: Wheelchair accessible unit overlooking the harbour. Cable, laundry, barbecues, and some kitchen units. (250) 726-4624. Box 614, 140 Bay Street.

LITTLE BEACH RESORT: Cabins with kitchen, ocean view, and cable. Close to local beaches and trails. (250) 726-4202. Box 730, 1187 Peninsula Road.

PACIFIC COAST COTTAGES: Cottages nestled among the hemlocks located on Highway 4 (Pacific Rim Highway) on the way into Ucluelet. (250) 726-4247. Box 104, 2415 Pacific Rim Highway.

PACIFIC RIM MOTEL: Close to shopping and restaurants. Cable and direct-dial phones. Some kitchen units available. (250) 726-7728. Box 173, 1755 Peninsula Road.

PENINSULA MOTOR INN: Located in central Ucluelet within walking distance of shops. Chinese and Western cuisine restaurant. (250) 726-7751. Box 433, 1648 Peninsula Road.

SHEILA'S COUNTRY COTTAGES: Quiet "country" atmosphere, near Ucluelet. One-bedroom cottages with full kitchen, living room, and full bath. (250) 726-4655. Box 284, 2425 Pacific Rim Highway.

THORNTON MOTEL: Sleeping and housekeeping units. Suites accommodate up to six. Small pets allowed. (250) 726-7725. Box 490, 1861 Peninsula Road.

UCLUELET HOTEL: Central Ucluelet, sleeping units with or without private bath. Lounge, pub, coffee shop, and licensed dining room. No phones or TV. (250) 726-4324. Box 10, 250 Main Street.

WEST COAST MOTEL: Indoor pool, squash court, sauna, exercise room, restaurant with view. Some in-room whirlpool baths. (250) 726-7732. Box 275, 247 Hemlock Street.

WATERFRONT COTTAGE: Cedar shake cottage situated on inlet's edge. Marine life view from handcrafted wooden interior. Close to shops, trails, and beaches. No smoking. Rowboat available. (250) 726-4203. Box 1092, 1533 Imperial Lane.

CAMPING

ISLAND WEST RESORT: Waterfront location, moorage and launching, fishing, diving, and tour charters available. (250) 726-7515. Box 614, 160 Hemlock Street.

LONG BEACH GOLF COURSE: Wilderness camping, portable toilets, near Pacific Rim National Park Reserve. (250) 725-3332. Box 998, Pacific Rim Highway.

MUSSEL BEACH CAMPGROUND: Twenty minutes from Ucluelet / Tofino Junction on the north side of Barkley Sound. (250) 537-2081, Barkley Sound, B.C.

UCLUELET CAMPGROUND: Harbour waterfront, walking distance to shops and restaurants. Boat launch and moorage nearby. (250) 726-4355. Box 614, 260 Seaplane Base Road.

CHARTERS AND RECREATION

CANADIAN PRINCESS RESORT: Fishing and whale-watching tours. (250) 726-7771. Box 939, 1943 Peninsula Road.

CAR-MA-JEN SURF SHOP: Surf reports, surf and body board sales and rentals, wet suits, accessories, and lessons for all ages. (250) 726-2322. Box 79, 270 Main Street.

FIRST STRIKE CHARTERS: Salmon, halibut, and cod fishing, plus Barkley Sound nature tours. (250) 726-2028. Box 618, Ucluelet, B.C.

ISLAND TOURS: Charter boat services. Fishing, whale-watching, and nature tours. (250) 726-2050 or 726-7385. Box 1095, Ucluelet, B.C.

ISLAND WEST RESORT: Fishing, whale-watching, nature tours, and moorage. (250) 726-7515. Box 614, 140 Bay Street.

LONG BEACH GOLF COURSE: Nine holes, par 72, slope rating 116. Pro Shop, lounge/restaurant, meeting room, driving range, and putting green. (250) 725-3332. Box 998, Pacific Rim Highway.

MV LEGEND CHARTERS: 12.6-metre troller. Experienced West Coast fisher. Fishing and Broken Group Islands tours. (250) 726-7366. Box 1041, Ucluelet, B.C.

MAJESTIC KAYAKING: Kayak tours of Barkley and Clayoquot Sounds. (250) 726-2868. Box 287, Ucluelet, B.C.

QUEST CHARTERS: Full-service fishing charters. Experienced guides. (250) 726-7532. Box 487, Ucluelet, B.C.

RAVEN TOURS: Circle tours of Ucluelet, Pacific Rim National Park Reserve, and Tofino. (250) 726-7772. Box 161, Ucluelet, B.C.

SEATALE CHARTERS: Full-service guided fishing trips. (250) 726-2550. Box 203, 1636 Davison Plaza #6.

SUBTIDAL ADVENTURES: Diving, whale-watching, and nature tours. (250) 726-7336. Box 78, 1960 Peninsula Road.

GALLERIES

DUQUAH GALLERY: Native art, jewellery, and framing. (250) 726-7223. 1971 Peninsula Road.

MYSTIC HORIZON: Gifts, gallery, books, music, and flowers. (250) 726-7315. 1790 Peninsula Road.

THIRSK GALLERY AND ARTFOLK SUPPLIES: Gallery, arts and crafts supplies. (250) 726-2012. 272 Main Street.

EMERGENCY SERVICES

POLICE / FIRE / AMBULANCE: 911.
POLICE (nonemergency calls): (250) 726-7773.
HOSPITAL (Tofino General): (250) 725-3212. 261 Neill Street, Tofino.

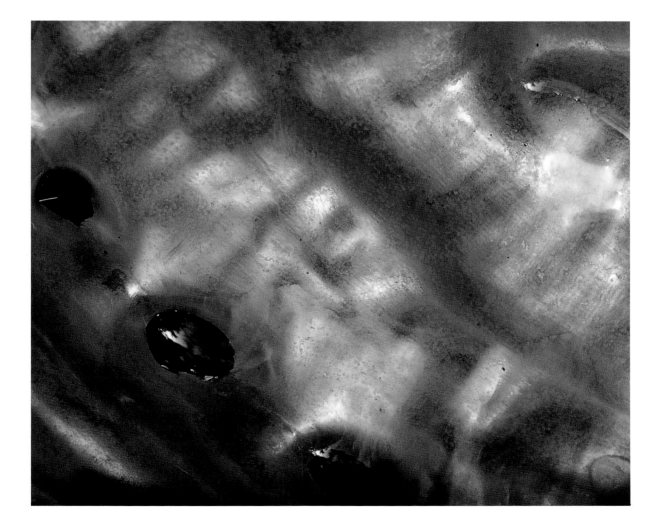

Selected Reading

Andersen, Marnie. *Women of the West Coast: Then and Now*. Sidney,
    B.C.: Sand Dollar Press, 1993.

Coull, Cheryl. *A Traveller's Guide to Aboriginal B.C.* North Vancouver:
    Whitecap Books, 1996.

George, Paul, et. al. *Meares Island: Protecting a Natural Paradise*.
    Tofino, B.C.: Friends of Clayoquot Sound and Western
    Canada Wilderness Committee, 1985.

Gill, Ian. *Hiking on the Edge: Canada's West Coast Trail*. Vancouver:
    Raincoast Books, 1995.

Kozloff, Eugene N. *Seashore Life of the Northern Pacific Coast*. Seattle:
    University of Washington Press, 1983.

MacFarlane, J. M., et al. *The Official Guide to Pacific Rim National Park
    Reserve*. Calgary: Blackbird Naturgraphics, 1996.

MacIsaac, Ron, and Anne Champagne, eds. *Clayoquot Mass Trials:
    Defending the Rainforest*. Philadelphia: New Society Publishers,
    1994.

McConnaghey, Bayard H., and Evelyn McConnaghey. *National
    Audubon Society Field Guide to North American Birds*. New York:
    Knopf, 1985.

Obee, Bruce. *The Pacific Rim Explorer*. North Vancouver: Whitecap
    Books, 1986.

Walbran, Capt. John T. *British Columbia Coast Names 1592–1906:
    Their Origin and History*. Vancouver: J. J. Douglas, 1971.

Young, Nat. *Surfing Fundamentals*. Los Angeles: Body Press, 1985.

*Technicolor brilliance of intertidal life: green sea
anemones and an orange sunflower starfish
share a Long Beach tide pool.*

NEXT PAGE:
*Changing of the guard: after the
sun goes down on Canada, a summer's moon
stands watch over Chesterman Beach.*

Notes on the Photography

Bob Herger took his first photograph of Long Beach 30 years ago when he attempted to duplicate the cover of the Beach Boys album *Surfing Safari,* the one featuring a Woody station wagon on a beach crowded with Beach Boys. With as many friends as he could stuff into his red Austin Mini, Bob drove to Long Beach and took that memorable first photograph with a brand-new Kodak Instamatic 126 camera.

Things have changed a lot since that frivolous summer day, the most obvious being that you can no longer drive onto Long Beach. Bob's equipment has changed, too. For this book he used Nikon cameras and 35 mm Fuji Velvia 50 film, and carried lenses that ranged from 16 mm to 300 mm in a Lowe Pro backpack-type case. As for tripods, he often used a medium-weight Manfrotto when wandering along the beach or clambering over rocky outcroppings.

Bob says that one of the chief challenges in photographing the Long Beach area is keeping the inside of your camera clean. Even getting one grain of sand lodged in the film take-up mechanism of your camera can ruin a roll of film. He suggests cleaning the inside of the camera with blasts of canned air after every roll change.

Surfing is even more popular at Long Beach these days, and the Beach Boys are still around more or less, but Bob's Austin is long gone. So is the Instamatic.

BRIAN PAYTON *(left)* has written for numerous publications, including *Islands*, the *New York Times*, and the *Globe and Mail*. He also co-wrote *Spirit Transformed: A Journey from Tree to Totem* with internationally acclaimed Canadian artist Roy Henry Vickers and is the author of the forthcoming *Cowboy*. He now lives on Denman Island in British Columbia.

BOB HERGER *(right)*, one of Canada's foremost photographers, has had his award-winning work featured in *National Geographic*, *Time*, *Sierra*, and *Newsweek*. His books include *The Coast of British Columbia*, *The Forests of British Columbia*, and the recently published *Spirit Transformed: A Journey from Tree to Totem*. He currently lives with his family in Maple Ridge, British Columbia.

COVER PHOTOS BY BOB HERGER

DESIGNED BY DEAN ALLEN

PRINTED AND BOUND IN CHINA